LoveLines

part of the
Perfect Words Worth Repeating
series

by
Linda LaTourelle

Bluegrass
PUBLISHING
mayfield ky

For information write:
Blue Grass Publishing
PO Box 634
Mayfield, KY 42066 USA
service@theultimateword.com
www.bluegrasspublishing.com
www.theultimateword.com

ISBN: 0-9761925-9-4

1st ed.
Mayfield, KY : Blue Grass Pub., 2005

Blue Grass Publishers has made every effort to give proper ownership credit for all poems and quotes used within this book. In the event of a question arising from the use of a poem or quote, we regret any error made and will be pleased to make the necessary correction in future editions of this book. All scripture was taken from the King James Version of the Bible.

Cover Design: Todd Jones, Tennessee
Proudly printed in the United States of America

10 9 8 7 6 5 4 3 2 1

LoveLines

Perfect Words Worth Repeating

Linda LaTourelle has married words and artistic flair in "LoveLines", the first book in its newest series entitled "Perfect Words Worth Repeating©". Whether it is a first crush, or the fiftieth wedding anniversary, "LoveLines" will have a selection to help express just the right feeling to those you love. A compilation of more than 500 traditional and original romantic quotes, poems, songs and sayings, "LoveLines" gives its users more than just words from which to choose. Each selection is a work of art!

We know you'll have fun designing your own love creations with this one of a kind collection. After all love isn't love until you give it away! Just think how it will bless someone with a handmade sentiment created especially for them!

These carefully selected LoveLines will not only embellish your creations with style and romance, but you may also declare your love with their timeless beauty of heartfelt prose and poetry. They are certain to give your project a design you are proud to share.

LoveLines are ready to use. For example, you can customize your work by...

o   Copying the LoveLine onto vellum or your favorite paper for use on any project

o   Scanning the LoveLine to your computer, then manipulate it to fit your project

o   Recreating the phrase manually or in your favorite software.

Whether you are a Scrapbooker, Stamper or Cardmaker, we're certain you'll be reaching for this great collection time and again. Linda LaTourelle has a knack for finding the words, quotes and phrases you've been looking for before you even know that you are looking for them. The Perfect Words Worth Repeating© series from our best selling ULTIMATE line of books is both economical and priceless, tailor-made to inspire you on to greatness! We know you'll discover these are the *perfect words worth repeating*. Bluegrass Publishing has more books in this series coming soon. Be sure to visit your local stores or our website (www.bluegrasspublishing.com) for our entire ULTIMATE line.

LoveLines

is dedicated to
my beautiful
daughters.

It is their love
that makes my life
so blessed. Through
them I have learned to
love unconditionally.
Everyday they teach me
what love really means.

My dear daughters
you are truly the
essence of
Love.

Because of you I am a better person.
I am so very proud of the phenomenal
young ladies you are growing up to be.
I am blessed beyond belief.
I Love You both with all my heart.
Thank You.

Thank you to the Lord
for all of His blessings.
It is by His grace that I am
able to share my passion with you.
May you be filled with the ultimate love
of the one who loves you most.
And in return may you
love others the way
He loves you.

*Oh how He Loves
You and Me*

Love never fails

1 Corinthians 13:8

From the very
first moment
I beheld you,
my heart
was irrevocably
gone

—Jane Austen

Dance me
to the
end of
Love

My love for you is a journey;

starting at Forever

And ending at never

Love
You

making memories of Love

You

If you live to be a hundred.
I want to live to be
a hundred minus one day.
So I never have to live
a day without you

TILL THE END OF TIME

6

Love puts the fun in together,
The sad in apart,
The hope in tomorrow,
The joy in the heart.

The best portion of a good man's life, is his little, nameless, unremembered acts of kindness and LOVE.

-William Wordsworth

There is no **end**.
There is no *beginning*.
There is only the *infinite*
passion of
Love

-Federico Fellini

Adorable

i am not looking for someone i can live with, but the one i can not live without.

true Love

let me call you
sweetheart

If, out of time,
I could pick ONE moment and
keep it **shining** always new,
of all the days that I have lived,
I'd pick the moment I met you

There's only
me ♥ you

*Being in love is a patchwork of
a thousand indescribable moments.*

i Love Your FUNNY FACE

LOVE

Grow old with me the best is yet to be.
-Robert Browning

I do delight in thy Love

May no gift be too small to give, nor too simple to receive, which is wrapped in thoughtfulness and tied with love.
~L.O. Baird

and two shall become one

I have learned not to worry about LOVE but to honor its coming with all my HEART

Love Dance

My King

King of the castle

MY LOVE

My Fairytale came true the day I met YOU

Prince of my Heart

Roses
Are Red
Violets
Are
Blue
Sugar is
Sweet
And
I
Love
You

Sugar Pie, Honey Bunch

I
Love
You
a
bushel
and
a peck
and
a
hug
around
the
neck

Honey
Bun

SUGAR
SUGAR

WHEN i THINK of YOU i THINK happy

naughty

My
My Man
Love

I LOVE YOU IN A
PLACE WHERE THERE'S NO
SPACE OR TIME

Eternity

Heaven's
Kiss

Together
Forever

Love
Is in the air

Forever My Love

KING OF MY HEART

I GOT YOU BABE

Shadow of your smile

You stole my heart

Being deeply loved by someone gives you strength. Loving someone deeply gives you courage. —Lao Tzu

BEST Friends

Because you loved me

one in a million

Beloved

Oh my
Love's
like a red, red rose,
that's newly
sprung in June;
Oh my love's like
the melody
that's sweetly
played in tune.
~Robert Burns

16

I'm in the mood for

Love

How sweet it is!

How wonderful
How marvelous
is your precious
Love for me

wonderful
marvelous
precious

How sweet it is!

Love Bug

The Look of

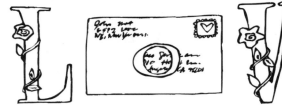

L O V E

When a man
Loves
a woman

You look beautiful tonight!

To Love
and be Loved
is to feel the sun
from both sides

Sweet

Adoration

He Loves Me
He Loves Me Not

A Fool in Love

Roses are red, violets are blue.

P.S. I LOVE YOU

just the two of US

Afternoon Delight

Heartthrob

I just called to say

I LOVE YOU

Love, Love we do
Our **LOVE** is so *true*

Sugar baby

Lovin' you–loving me

a GOOD MARRIAGE is at least
80% percent good luck in finding
THE RIGHT PERSON at the right time.
The rest is TRUST
-Nanette Newman

My Heart is yours
FOREVER

Soul Duet

When I count my blessings
I count you daily in my prayers!

Recipe for Love

have I told you lately that I love you?

22

Your LOVE to me is pure JOY

So Sweet!

That old feeling

Lovers

So Happy Together

Hopelessly devoted to you

Baby I'm yours

Amorè

Bear Hugs

Poetry In Motion

Little Darling

Lost in the Loving

Standin' on the corner watchin' all the girls go by

A kiss to build a dream on

YOUR KISS YOUR KISS IS ON MY HEART

innocent

Sealed with a Kiss

Kisses sweeter than wine

First Kiss

Journeys end in Lover's meeting

Together

just YOU
just ME
just right!

New Love

Soul Mates

Let me call you SWEETHEART

I never knew

Until I knew you

Our Love
a Circle without end
FOREVER

Still the One

a kiss is
a rosy dot
over the i
in loving

Love

Love is...

Back in baby's arms

even the nights are better

It had to be you

The
Very
Thought
of
YOU

All
I have to
do is
DREAM

Love bade me welcome,
but my soul drew back

-George Herbert

Moments to Remember

Someone to watch over me

love of my life

One **Love** That will last **FOREVER**

Tea for two

Be my little sugar
and love me forever more

Catch a falling star

Stardust

It's only make believe

Some enchanted evening

YOU
hung
the
moon

I'm sending
you some kisses
to remember
My Love

MY ONE AND ONLY

Only In My Dreams

Baby I'm I'm Yours

Do you think I'm I'm sexy?

Every **breath** I take

soulmate; 1. noun: someone for whom one has a deep connection and passion, esp. a lover, wife, husband, etc.; 2. n. a best friend; 3. n. the one

You belong to Me

Through the years
Through all the good and bad
Your love has made me glad

A little bit more

LoveLines

The **best** thing **to hold** onto in this world is **each other.**

–Linda Ellerbee

The story of US

I will always love you

ᵃWiNK, & ᵃSMiLE

Once upon a time...

Forever & Always

34

Come Away With Me

CLOSE to YOU

The More I See You

The Nearness of You

I'm Yours

I'm my beloved's and he is mine

A **Groovy** Kind of Love

If I had a
flower
for every time
I thought of you
I could walk in my
garden
forever

-Alfred Lord Tennyson

If ever two were one,
then surely we.
If ever man were
loved by wife,
then thee.

-Anne Bradstreet

36

Love simply iS

My eyes adored him

Can't Stop Loving You

Love
at first sight
is easy to understand
It's when
two people
have been
looking at each other
for years
that it becomes a
miracle

-Sam Levenson

LOVE STORY

When I fall in love it will be forever

If I ever write the story of my life don't be surprised if you're where it begins

MY LOVE

It was a deep and desperate time-need,
a clock ticking within his heart,
and it urged him,
against the whole logic of his life,
to walk past her into the house
now and say,
"This is forever."

-F. Scott Fitzgerald

Simply Irresistable

Moonlight Serenade

We loved
with a love
that was more than
LOVE

-Edgar Allan Poe

You
Belong to
Me

And I fell
n

with you

In the wee small hours of the morning

Lover Boy

Moonstruck

Irresistible

Fooled around and fell in Love

THESE foolish things

Pillow Talk

Beautiful!

All for Love

I was nauseous
and tingly all over.
I was either in love
or I had smallpox

What is love?
It is the morning and the evening star.

If passion holds you,
let reason drive the reins

A kiss when all is said
My heart whispering to yours

Love Thoughts

Naughty and Nice

Romantic Rendezvous

Makin' Whoopee

PUPPY LOVE

Dream Lover

With this Ring

True Love

Your body
is a wonderland
of love to me

You had me at hello

Though ocean's apart
you live in my heart

Our love is beautiful

You and Me

Breathless

'S Wonderful

Mon Chéri Je t'aime

French for: My darling, I love you

I've loved you forever
in lifetimes before

Begin the Beguine

A "Beguine" is a dance similar to the Rumba and is also the name of the music for it.

To see her is to love her,
And love but her forever;
For nature made her what she is,
And never made another!

–Robert Burns

If I could be
in two places
at one time,
I'd be
with you
twice,
all the time

Starry
Eyed

Snuggle Up
& Kiss
Me

I'm
in the
mood for
LOVE

Love sacrifices all things to bless the thing it loves!
-Lytton

I'm in the mood for
LOVE

Blessed is the influence of one true loving soul on another.
-George Elliot

Unforgettable

Just
Me
and
You

I love you
I love you
I love you
It's True!

One is never too old for romance.

Crazy in Love

The light that lies
in my beloveds eyes
has been my heart's undoing

Hot Stuff

There is no living with thee,
nor without thee

What a WONDERFUL World

A book of verse, underneath the bough,
jug of wine, a loaf of bread and thou
Beside me singing in the wilderness
Ah, wilderness were paradise now!
-Omar Khayam

He's so fine

Me & Thee

i wanna be around for the rest of your life

Once he drew with one long *kiss* my whole soul through my lips as sunlight drinketh dew.
—Tennyson

all for love

Pretty woman

Just one Kiss

I have found the one my soul loves

LoveLines

He is the one who
makes me smile
Making each day so worthwhile
He is my moon, my stars and sun
Deep in my heart
he is the only one.

YOU CHANGED
MY WORLD
WITH JUST
one kiss

my love
your love
our love

You
are
loved

Written on
the pages deep within
My HEART
you've been my TRUE
LOVE STORY
right from
the very start

Wild nights—Wild nights!
Were I with thee
Wild nights should be
Our luxury!
Futile—the winds—
To a heart in port—
Done with the compass—
Done with the chart!

Rowing in Eden—
Ah, the sea!
Might I but moor—Tonight—
In Thee!

-Emily Dickinson

Babe

Totally Yours

MY
ONE
TRUE
LOVE

All of me
Darling
take all of me

Yours

Accept the things to which fate binds you and love the people with whom fate brings you together... but do so with all your HEART

-Marcus Aurelius

my memories of LOVE will be of YOU

Love is a sheltering tree

Love makes the world go round

My Heart's Desire

Lyin' in your Loving arms at last

Mornin' Beautiful!

My eyes Adore You

My lover, my friend my life

the measure of our Love is that we love without measure Love

Do you love me?

Heart of My Heart

The Sweetness of love

He press'd his hand in slumber, so once more

She could not help but Kiss him and adore.

—John Keats

Every Jack must have his Jill.

Love

beareth all things
believeth all things
hopeth all things
endureth all things...
1 Corinthians 13:8

If I tell you
I LOVE YOU
can I keep you
FOREVER?

BABYCAKES

We had a lot in common
I loved him and he loved me

Heaven Sent

Those who give love, gather love

some kind of
WONDERFUL

To be is to love,
    to love you is to be

All is fair in love and war.
-Francis Edward Smedley

Soulmates

The **Man** I love

LOVE ME LITTLE
LOVE ME LONG
TIS THE MELODY
OF MY SONG

MY BOYFRIENDS BACK

But his kiss was so sweet
and so closely he pressed?
that I languished and pined
till I granted the rest.
— John Gay

57

I Love thee
to the depth and breadth
and height my SOUL
can reach
-Browning

My
Diamond
in the rough

Wild Nights

Love heals the soul and mends hearts

Love starts with a smile
grows with a kiss
and ends with a tear

58

My bounty is as boundless as the sea,
my love is deep, the more I give to thee
the more I have, for both are infinite
                                        -Shakespeare

Passion

For Love is me and you!

The soul that can *speak*
with its *eyes*
can also *kiss*
with a *gaze*

O, spirit of
Love
how quick and fresh
art thou.
                -Shakespeare

A boy
is holding
a girl
so very
tight
in his
arms
tonight.

                -Edward, Duke of Windsor

For
LOVE reflects
the thing
BELOVED

-Tennyson

PROMISE

Love is a promise that is always kept,
a fortune that can never be spent,
a seed that can flourish
in even the most unlikely of places.
And this radiance that never fades,
this mysterious and magical joy,
is the greatest treasure of all
one known only by those who love.

GREATEST

LOVE

A thing of beauty is joy forever.

-John Keats

Never go to bed mad
Stay up and fight.

-Phyllis Diller

60

i love you
and
you
love
me

the hardest things
in the world
are overcome with
LOVE

Smooch

There's this place in me where
your fingerprints still rest,
your kisses still linger
and your whispers softly echo.
It's the place where a part of you
will forever be a part of me.
-Gretchen Kemp

The most
precious possession
that ever comes to a Man
in this world is a woman's
heart

Beautiful Dreamer

Fly me to the moon

You are my everything

The Love of my life

Happiness is being in love with your best friend

Come
let us take our fill of *Love*
until the morning:
let us *Delight*
ourselves with
Love
—Proverbs 7:18

The summer hath his joys,
And winter his delights;
Though love and his pleasures
are but toys,
They shorten tedious nights.
—Thomas Campion

Would you dance? Dance
Would you hold me tight?

There may be many flowers
in a man's life, but there is only

one rose

Other men it is said have seen angels,
but I have seen thee and thou art enough.
-George Moore

Soul meets soul on lover's lips
- Shelly

I found the one
whom my soul loves
I held him and would
not let him go
-Song of Solomon 3:4

The Glory Of Love

Sweet Nothings

When
I
Fell
In love
With
YOU
All
My
Dreams
Came
true

Love
is the beginning
the middle
and the end
of everything.
-Lacordaire

Nothing
compares
to the touch
of your love
on my heart!

Many waters cannot quench love, neither can floods drown it.

Song of Solomon 8:7

He says
She says

Love is
that condition
in which
the happiness of another person
is essential to your own.

-Robert Heinlein

Till
all the seas go dry
my dear
and the rocks melt with the sun
I will love thee still
my dear
while the sands
of life shall run

ONE IS NEVER TOO OLD FOR ROMANCE

a Lover is someone who knows the song in your Heart and can Sing it back to you when You have forgotten the Words

I like your body when it is with my body...

-e.e. cummings

To Know you is to Love you

And they lived...

HAPPILY
EVER AFTER

Do you love me
    because I am beautiful?
Or am I beautiful
    because you love me?

Life is a flower of which

LOVE IS THE HONEY

Thou art to me
a delicious torment

Dream

Lover

Perfect

Baby

Baby

how you

hear my

heartbeat!

Today & Forever

you are SPECIAL

Your love is pure
EMOTION

Dream

Love in Bloom

Women still remember the first kiss
after men have forgotten the last.
    —Gourmont

Come live with me, and be my love,
And we will some new pleasures prove
Of golden sands, and crystal brooks,
With silken lines, and silver hooks.
                —John Donne

For it was not into
my ear you whispered,
but into my heart.
It was not my lips
you kissed, but my soul.

First Love

I want all of your Love
You're a gift from above
All your joys and all your sorrows
Your todays and your tomorrows

Hot Legs

Keeper of my Stars

I love her
and that's the beginning
of everything
-F. Scott Fitzgerald

Anyone can be passionate
but it takes real **Lovers**
to be **silly**
-Rose Dorothy Franken

The way you look tonight

The *Rose* speaks of love silently in a language known only to the **Heart**

whisper words of love

In dreams and in **Love** there are no impossibilities

You're nothing short of my **EVERYTHING**

Love is friendship set on fire

The only gift is a portion of thyself.
— *Emerson*

FOR YOU

With all my LOVE

SWeet KiSSeS

LoveLines

The sunlight claps the earth
and the moonbeams kiss the sea,
what are all these kissings worth
if thou kiss not me?

-Percey Bysshe Shelley

Heartbeat

True poets
don't write
Their thoughts
with a pen...
They release
the ink that
flows from
within their
heart

TRUE LOVE

Paradise
is always
where love dwells
Paradise is
you and me
together

Addicted to
Love
Addicted to
You

Lover's are like stars
There's millions of them,
But only one can make
all of your dreams come true

Need I say more?

I am your canvas
paint me with your
Love

LoveLines

The first time
I saw you
I kissed
my heart goodbye

Falling in love is when
he lays in your arms
and wakes up in your dreams

Will you meet me in my
DREAMS?

In the absence of
Love there is nothing
worth fighting for

—Elijah Wood

That though the radiance which was once so bright be now forever taken from my sight. Though nothing can bring back the hour of splendor in the grass, glory in the flower. We will grieve not, rather find strength in what remains behind.

-Wordsworth

I may not be a smart man, but I know what love is.

-Forest Gump

i found my knight in shining armor

you & me

77

Written on my Heart

You know *you are in* love
when you can't sleep *at night*
because real life is better
than *your* dreams.

Forever, I Do

The magic of first Love is believing in happily ever after

All you need is love.
-John Lennon

I need him like I need the air to breathe

I only thought about you once today I just never stopped

Sometimes the heart sees what is invisible to the eye.

LOVE
is just
a word
'til
you meet
that
ONE
special
person

YOU
are what
happened
when I wished
upon a STAR

Do ALL things
with LOVE

Once **in awhile**
right in the middle of
an ordinary life,
love gives us a
Fairytale

You

My Hero

My Darling

The HEART
holds onto things
the mind forgets

call Me: 911-LOVE

A kiss is just a kiss
until it's someone you love

When you love someone
time is Eternity

The most
eloquent silence;
that of two mouths
meeting in a kiss.

An affair to remember

From this moment on

Love means never having
to say you're sorry.
-Kyle Schmidt

These Foolish Things

Love Will Find a Way

I don't want to be **something** to everyone, just **everything** to you

You are the sun
in my winter sky,
you are the hello
in my good-bye.
You are the stars
shining down on me.
You are everything
I had hoped you'd be.
You are the arms
wrapped around a hug;
you are the pull when
I need a little tug.
You are the lips that feel
my gentle touch;
you are the one
who loves me so much.
You are the one
who I come to for love;
you are my angel from above.
I need your love;
I need you too,
simply said
I am the I in
I LOVE YOU.

-Linda LaTourelle

I love thee, I love but thee
With a love that shall not die
Till the sun grows cold
And the stars grow old.

–William Shakespeare

Love builds bridges
where there
are none.

–Comte DeBussy–Rabutin

Kisses in the morning
Loving all the day

Sweetheart

Where there is love there is life.

–Erich Fromm

Talk
not of wasted affection
Affection was never wasted
—Longfellow

Love

And the Lord God said,
"It is not good
that man should be alone;
I will make him a help mate."

—Genesis 2:18

You made me love you

till the end of never

Isn't it Romantic?

SO FALL ASLEEP LOVE
LOVED BY ME,
FOR I KNOW LOVE,
I AM LOVED BY THEE.
-ROBERT BROWNING

Shall we dance

Life isn't measured by
how many breaths you take,
but by what takes your
breath away.

A relationship is like a rose
how long it lasts, no one knows
Love can erase an awful past
Love can be yours, you'll see at last
to feel that love, it makes you sigh
to have it leave you'd rather die
You hope you've found that special rose
'cause you love and care
for the one you chose. -Willa Cather

BLESSED
IS THE HOME
WHERE YOU PUT EACH
OTHER'S HAPPINESS FIRST
-KENDRA

The sweetest joy
The wildest woe is
Love

-Philip Bailey

Marriage is like the army.
Everybody complains,
but you'd be surprised
at how many re-enlist.

sentimental journey

Your love is the rythmn in my heart

LOVE

Our love is a circle that begins with

Me & You

Love is friendship set to MUSic

For hearing my thoughts understanding my dreams and being my friend. For filling my life with joy and loving me without end.

Friend

A white sportcoat
& a pink carnation

Blushing
Bride

I only have
eyes for
YOU

Love
does not consist of
gazing at
each other
But looking outward
in the same direction
-Antoine deSaint-Exupery

My First, My Last, My Everything

89

Today, Tomorrow & Forever

Let us love
one another
for **Love**
comes from God
-1 John 4:7

Only Love
let's us see
ordinary things as
extraordinary

Love one another
deeply from the heart
-1Peter 1:22

I am yours & you are mine

The Lord watch between me and thee when we are absent from each other

-Genesis 31:49

many things in life will catch your eye, but only one will catch your **HEART**

Love is an
OCEAN of EMOTIONS,
entirely surrounded by
EXPENSES.
~Thomas Dewar

Love
is
better
the second
time
-Vern

Love is the triumph of imagination over intelligence

Love is a fabric which never fades,
no matter how often it is washed
in the water of adversity and grief.
~Author Unknown

 **W**here there is
great love,
there are always

wishes.
-Leo Buscaglia

Our hearts echo from
soul to soul
reaching deep
and making us whole
-Linda LaTourelle

There is no instinct
like that of the
HEART

Kindred Spirits

You MAKE
MY HEART
Sing

our fairytale
is the beginning
of forever

in the storms
of our
love
may we
always dance
in the rain
together

The word
Love

WE

can be explained in thousands
of ways, but the only word that
comes to mind is

YOU!

The mark of a true crush is that you fall in love first and grope for reasons ...afterward

The art of Love is the art of persistence

-T.S. Elliot

Wrapped in Love with You

Thank you for the Love you give to Me every day Thank you for the Love that teaches Me the way Thank you God above for filling our home with extraordinary LOVE

Thanks

ITS YOU AND ME

This was love at first sight,
love everlasting,
a feeling unexpected;
it took entire possession
of him and he understood
with joyous amazement
that this was for life.
—Thomas Mann

Girlfriend

Boyfriend

If ever there comes a day
when we can't be together
Keep me in your heart,
I'll stay there forever
-Pooh

forever

Through the eyes of your love

What the heart gives away
is never gone ...
it is kept
in the hearts of others.
-Robin St. John

Forever

The first time I saw you
I kissed
my heart good bye

Tis you alone that sweetens life...

TIME IS...
too slow for those who wait,
too swift for those who grieve,
too short for those who rejoice,
but for those who love...
time is ETERNITY

ETERNITY

What is there in life...but LOVE?

Love YOU all over again

I love your feet because they walked upon the earth until they found me.

tootsies

You are the SUNSHINE of my Life

Love is the beauty of the Soul

The course of true love
never did run smooth

-William Shakespeare

Alas!
the love of women---it is known
To be a lovely
and fearful thing! ~Lord Byron

What I feel for you
seems less of earth and
more of a cloudless heaven.

you

-Victor Hugo

Where your treasure is
there your heart will be also

-Matthew 6:21

Love shared is joy doubled

Tweet hearts

When Love & skill work **Together** expect a miracle

Grow old *with me* the best *is yet to be* best

Loving you makes me dizzy or else my blonde is showing too much

Symphony of Love

The song of love
is your breath upon my lips
and the rhythm of
your heart against mine.
You are the music
that resonates deep
within my soul.
You are my
symphony of love.

**What we have once enjoyed
we can never lose.
All that we love deeply
becomes a part of us.**
—Helen Keller

heart

The human heart, at whatever age,
opens to the heart that opens in return.
~Maria Edgeworth

Love betters what is Best!

How SWEET the words of truth
when breathed softly from the lips of

LOVE

Something old
Something new,
Something borrowed
Something blue

I wrote your name in the sand,
but the waves washed it away
Then I wrote it in the sky,
but the wind blew it away.
So I wrote it in my heart,
and there it will forever stay.

The
first
time
ever
I kissed
your
lips
I was
yours

Love is the creator of our favorite memories and the foundation of our fondest dreams.

love is all there is

so sexy

He gave her a look you could have poured on a waffle.
-Ring Lardner

marriage

Marriage made in Heaven

TWO...
are better than one

YOU bring out the BEST in me!

Only You

your
love is
a little
bit of
heaven
in
my
heart

I never knew how
to worship
until I knew how to
LOVE
-Henry Ward Beecher

And pure love—
why, some days
it's so quiet,
you don't even know
it's there.
~Erma Bombeck

If I could reach up and grab a **star** for every time you made me **smile** I'd have the entire night **sky** in the palm of my hand

I Love You

As the OCEAN is never FULL of water so is the heart never full of LOVE

Real Love Stories never have endings.

The love that we have in our youth is superficial compared to the love that an old man has for his old wife.

-Will Durant

So, fall asleep, love, loved by me...for I know love, I am loved by thee.

-Robert Browning

When you came you were like
red wine and honey,
and the taste of you
burnt my mouth
with it's sweetness.
Now you are like morning bread,
smooth and pleasant.
I hardly taste you at all
for I know your savour,
but I am completely nourished.

-Amy Lowell

Our love is so furious... -Richard Burton to Elizabeth Taylor

Love does not begin and end the way we seem to think it does Love is a battle, Love is a war Love is growing up.

Lovin you

I saw his eyes and I was swept away. I heard his voice and I smiled that whole day. I touched his hand and my body felt helpless. I learned about his soul and my mind drifted away.

Tenderness

I've loved you forever, in lifetimes before.

Love

What is love?
No one can define it.
It's something so great,
only God could design it.
Love is beyond what man can define.
for love is immortal.
And God's gift is divine.

The road is bright before us,
as hand in hand we start.
We'll travel on
one mind,
one soul, together
one heart

My heart is yours

Thanks
for being my
Everything

I can still hear the song of your laughter

cupid

BE MINE

My funny
Valentine

Be my Valentine

We are
all born for *Love*
it is the principle existence
and it's only end.
—Disraeli

Thou art to me a delicious torment
—Emerson

Love is the essence of life

In our life there is a single color,
as on an artist's palette,
which proides
the meaning of life and art.
It is the Color of
LOVE
-Marc Chagall

Kiss Me

She walks in beauty
Like the night of cloudless climes
and starry skies
And all that's best
of dark and bright
Meet in her aspect and her
eyes

Our love is a journey that begins at forever & ends at never,

Love
LOVE
YOU
Forever

Honey

Je vous aimerai pour tous mes jours
I will love you for all of my days

Romance, ah sweet
Love
Romance!

Doubt that the stars are fire;
Doubt that the sun doth move;
Doubt truth to be a liar;
But never doubt I love.
—William Shakespeare

Love

I do, I do, I do Love You

At the
TOUCH OF LOVE
everyone becomes
A POET.
—Anaïs Nin

Baby Love

and now these three remain
FAITH, HOPE & LOVE
But the greatest of these is Love
—1 Corinthians 13:13

God
makes
all things possible
but
Love
makes
everything easier

first love

Romance
is the glamour
which turns
the dust of everyday life
into a golden haze.
-Elynor Glyn

To **Love**
another person
is to see the
face of
GOD

For those who love
time is eternity
eternity —Henry Van Dyke

You & Me
against the world

My Husband, My Friend

SUGAR Sugar in the morning
Sugar in the evening
Sugar all the time!

WILD THING,
HEART
you make my heart sing

Happiness
Happiness
is being married
to your Best Friend
Best Friend

True love is not what you get
but what you sacrifice to give away.
-Louis Izzo

Romantic

If you are asking if I need you
the answer is 4ever?
if you are asking if I will leave you,
the answer is never?
if you are asking what I value,
the answer is you!
if you are asking
if I love you
the answer is I do!

Here are our best sellers

and our newest creations...

Written by: Linda LaTourelle

Love Lines:
Artistic Quotes for Scrappers and Stampers NEW!

The Ultimate Guide to the Perfect Word
(ALL NEW...Vol. 2 coming Summer '05)

The Ultimate Guide to the Perfect Card
(Revised, coming in June '05) NEW!

The Ultimate Guide to Celebrating Kids Vol. 1

The Ultimate Guide to Celebrating Kids Vol. 2
(Coming in July '05) NEW!

The <u>largest</u> <u>collection</u> of poems & quotes ever created!

Written by: Thena Smith

Whispers: Passionate Poetry NEW!
Where's Thena? I need a poem about...

The reviews we have received in all the top magazines have been wonderful!
The feedback from stores and individuals is awesome!

The Perfect Words

Quotes, poems, titles, tips & more...
At your fingertips for any occasion, anytime!

▼

Bluegrass Publishing, Inc. has created
the **ULTIMATE** line of books
for all of your scrapbooking, stamping and cardmaking needs!

Many new products coming soon!
You can check out all our books
and products on our website.

www.bluegrasspublishing.com

Send us an e-mail: service@theultimateword.com

Order your book today?

Are you looking at your friend's book right now?
Great for gifts or just to read!

You can *mail* the order form below,
or you can *order online* at our website
or *call* us at **(270) 251-3600.**
Fax: (270) 251-3603

BLUEGRASS PUBLISHING
mail order form

Name		Date

Address

City/State/Zip

Credit Card #	E-mail

Exp. Date	Phone ( )

Qty	Title	Unit Cost	Total
	The Ultimate Guide to the Perfect Word	$19.95	
	"Perfect Words Worth Repeating"© Series (NEW)	▼	
	• LoveLines	$12.95	
	• A Mother's Heart/ A Father's Wisdom	$12.95	
	Whispers : Passionate Poetry and Words of Love (by Thena)	$12.95	
	Where's Thena? I need a poem about...	$19.95	
	The Ultimate Guide to Celebrating Kids Vol. 1	$19.95	
	The Ultimate Guide to Celebrating Kids Vol. 2 (NEW)	$19.95	
	The Ultimate Guide to the Perfect Card Revised (NEW)	$19.95	

Send order to:

BLUEGRASS PUBLISHING
PO Box 634
Mayfield, KY 42066

Subtotal		
Kentucky Tax 6 %		
Shipping (Per Book)	$2.95	
TOTAL	$	

Need a gift for a friend?

Order today!

All of our books are
great for gifts or just to read!

www.bluegrasspublishing.com
Phone (270) 251-3600
Fax (270) 251-3603
E-mail: service@theultimateword.com

For the best fonts ever go to:

Lettering Delights
www.letteringdelights.com
These <u>are</u> the font people! You can order online, too!

MAIL ORDER FORM: (*Send to address below)

Name	Date
Address	E-mail
City/State/Zip	
Credit Card #	
Exp. Date	Phone ( )

Qty	Title	Each	Total

Send order to:

Inspire Graphics
PO Box 935
Pleasant Grove, UT 84062

Subtotal	
Utah Tax 4.75%	
Shipping	
TOTAL	$

Thank you for your order